NEUTROPIA

Surrealistic Poetry

Al Case

Quality Press

copyright © 2024 by Alton H. Case

for information regarding this book go to:

AlCaseBooks.com
MonsterMartialArts.com

.

table of contents

introduction

I did not write
I was written.

Read this book one random page a day
and your mind will be connected.

Read a poem total and go sane
no matter how much it hurts.

Read the whole book
and sanity will stop confusing you.

Do not read this book
let it read you.

If you do not understand
let it read you again
until you are finally understood.

just this thought

sometimes i listen
ear to the trunk
i hear the ants crawling
the termites calling
the limbs waving
with creaks louder than a haunted house

life
it haunts me

and i listen
with an ear to the pipe of a rusty house
dissoluting
in need of repair from the beginning
for it is already dead

and when i am listening people speak to me
they tell me of their work and woes
and the myriad details
of which i am not interested

think:
life consists of actions of which i already know
as does everybody
who thinks
who looks
who knows

work is a series of things which must be done
fast and without error
and if you own the workers
the customers own you
work is a series of things which must be done
fast and without error

if you sell things
you must make a friend before you sell
that is the secret of life

we are all cogs in the same machine
and we must all get along
lest the machine chew us up

of course,
there is beyond hands
beyond hands,
beyond flesh,
beyond motor
beyond machine
a choice to disengage oneself
from the machine of the universe
and thus
to operate the machine of the universe

i listen to what is beyond hands
i listen to what is beyond flesh
beyond motor and machine

i listen to what is beyond the call of termites
as they build their empire
and as they fight the ants
and know not
they are just ants of a different stripe

i listen to the sound of a tree waving
and wonder to whom does it wave?
free of desire
unfurling in the wind
moving through the universe
each leaf
without moving

partaking of the wind
by letting the wind come

ahhhh,
the universe sighs
at last,
someone is listening

i listen.
i listen to those who listen
and the listening of listening
so far beyond machines
is the true purpose of the universe
and a blessing

i listen to winds of no air
sighing through the planets
singing celestial
space a bellows to propel the imagination
the sun a furnace to heat desire
and each planet a chime
a chime
a chime
and you,
the spirit,
sailing

to whence there is no flesh nor games
just the pureness of is and now

i listen
and the universe listens to me

i listen,
and am finally listened to

i listen
and out there
beyond hands
is finally something to listen to

if only the ants could listen to the termites
if only the termites could listen to the ants
if they could listen to each other
they would hear the same song

but it takes silence to listen,
and what termite could stop doing his doing
long enough to listen?

what ant could stop doing his doing
long enough to listen?

what silence could be born upon the wings
of the unborn imagination!

what listenings could be unfurled upon the universe!

then the machine would work
then the motors would turn
then the flesh would sing
and spirits would hum in tune to the chimes

then the universe would be happy
listened to
heeded
it's purpose fulfilled
just this thought is enough to make it so
listen

just this thought of ants and termites
realizing that they eat their own home
is enough to make the universe happy

just this thought
and the winds are ready to go

just this thought

listen
can you hear the far trees waiting?

can you hear us
singing ourselves from planet to planet?

can you hear?

judge not your fellow man
for that is an unlistening

hate not your fellow man
for that is not your true stripe
that is not your house
the one you truly live in

do not not in simple conversation
rather
do
and listen
and when your fellow man is listened to
he will see beyond hands

he will see
and go
and do
beyond hands

he will fill the universe with his song
singing in the silence of the soul electric
and he,
the soul,
free
to dance upon the wind of no air
between chimes and in tune with the purpose
of the universe and his existence

to imagine freely
to listen

i go now
i clap my hands and there is no sound

into no sound i listen even more carefully
until i am listened to

and when i am at last heard
when the universe hears my song complete
when all the trees have been unfurled
in all the airless winds of a myriad of uncounted planets

then
at last
will i be at peace

then
at last
will i have done what i was made for

then
at last
will i have made peace with myself

the trees undying will make houses
for the termites and the ants

the wind will sing the trees to a new breed of listeners
and the planets will chime to new skies
filled with listeners that always were

and i will listen
and when comes someone who listens for me
they will be heard

wisdom

take each word as it comes
take each thought as it is projected

take each day as it comes
take each life as it is projected

ah, all
if there is a god it is he
she, they, us

no one is excluded in our dreams
as we realize that we are dreams of each other

each other is us
consecrate in each other

each other is how we travel to the stars
to our depths
to our dreams

what is the universe but a dream?
and us the dreamers?

truth becomes a golden pastel
with which to paint the universe

truth becomes our every dream
and we become our dream

how do we fix the universe?
ask only if there is an answer

if there is no answer don't ask
and whatever you do
don't blame

blame is not responsibility
blame is not a correction
blame is not and shouldn't exist
rather ask
what now?
how now?
and do right
now
right now

if a child is born bless him
for he/she is a blessing

that child has blessed us
with his/her presence

a gift to help us set right the universe

if a man is crooked point not the finger
rather
help him help us set right the universe

if a woman is crooked condemn not
rather
ask her blessing
for she is the fount

if a man or woman is righteous
be kind in return
for they are blind.

if a man or woman is less than helpful
be patient
for they have not found themselves

man and woman balance the flow
and the universe is harmonious

or don't balance the flow
and the universe is not harmonious

creating children is easy
it's just a matter of spear and nest

raising children is a matter of balance
balanced flows create balanced children
unbalanced flows create monsters

there is your future
make it harmonious or not
as you wish

do not give yourself to an institution,
rather,
share in the universe
this is the secret of civilization

do not seek power for it is self defeating

seek,
rather,
competence
for that is self perpetuating

let power come only as a result of competence

remember
the parts are interchangeable

if a leader lies
change him

if a leader leaves what's right
change him

if a leader seeks power at the sacrifice of others
change him

to not change him
is let yourself be changed

the circle of family
the circle of friends
bow to the circle of man

no belief
no geography
no insanity
can separate the fact that we are
and we are together
no matter what

when a person exists in hatred
they have not flow
and will bow to those who do

there is not good nor bad
but rather
balance

if there is balance
you can exist in harmony
above concepts good or bad

the universe is a house for the spirit

spirit is dreams
spirit is what we are
spirit is forever

when all is balanced
when the planets spin and the suns glow
unhindered by ourselves
the game is done
until then...

play

circleverse

like a bird breaking through
it is swooping to the skies
fluttering to fall

it is a universe
circular
writhing
twisting
it turns upon itself
like the mind
it is a mirror

break through by breaking
that is one way
though it is fraught with peril

or,
look for the end of the mirror
it is imagination breaking through
on a lonely night you can see the stars

ah,
you can see
there is that hope
and once hoping
imagining on forever circles
that guide you through your lives

nothing you can do is bad
not even evil
you are what makes this universe
it is you
consecrate
flowing
creating
the ultimate god

like a dragon
you cry through the ages
your cry enlightens
turning and spiraling
in imitation dwindling
but not

how can you dwindle?
how can you shrink to disappear?
it is impossible
starkly impossible

like a phoenix rising
bursting through the clouds
lances of light in your hands
all enemies you slay

you are like a lion
roaring of pains and dreams and other fabrics
with which you twine yourself
playing the child's game of not being able
a lie in the face of what you are doing
what you are

turning like a crane
to see forever
wings spread to catch the light
feet stepping over mountains
and the universe is a thunderous ovation to your silence

i am all lives forever
there is no stopping me for i do not move
i move the universe and pretend it is me
this is the secret of circleverse

i am all lives
all lies
all eyes
all guise
all skies

like a tiger treading
stripes like shoots of bamboo hiding my motion
and when the wind waves
so do i
and i call it the wind
but it is me

none can stand before me

none can stand in this sky i call a home

none can stand but the others like me
who have gone home

circleverse is my home
it is me
lurching through the larger verse

circleverse is where i live
and you are welcome
for no harm can be done to it
to me
to us
as long as you are my guess

my quest is that every verse in the universe
be welcome in my circleverse

be welcome in me
i bear no harm
no ill will
no chilly wind

there is only me
warm and friendly and filled with lightening

would you like some of my lightening?
would you like to take what is mine?

dangerous now is the illusion
dangerous now is the verse

but it is you
you are the danger
for you are the mirror
which makes you a circleverse
and until you realize it
you are in danger

like a snake eating his tail
unable to regurgitate
fangs sinking
legless flailing
crying soundless
your verse is failing

come to mine
learn how to circle
how to turn upon yourself without harm

extend the hands in bridges of warm flow
bathe the universe

the universe likes you
you know
it likes being the mirror
for there is a joy within your mind

release the joy
soar
play like a monkey
frisky and chattering
the jungle suddenly your friend

we are your friend
realize that
know that
be that

the only enemy you have is not trusting yourself
trusting all the verses
climb to your heights

trusting circles until you never fall
never fail
trusting

trusting can never harm you
if you trust people to be exactly as they are

trust
that is the cement that holds us together
trust that can never be bent
we will do exactly as we promise
and the only lie
is not believing that

trust is our coin in a world beyond flesh
trust is our agreement
and there is no pain
except that caused by loss of trust.

can you find your trust?
can you sail the verse?
touch all the verses?
can you?

the answer is in circleverse
going far we find ourselves

going in we find our out
and the opposite is also true
i'm sure

going back we find our front

you can't back up in circleverse
for there are no roads
except those which lead to ourselves
to ourselves...

trust
find trust
and circle it upon yourself
give it to others freely
and you will be free

fluttering like a butterfly
unable to be struck in your agreement
you will find others

we like others in circleverse
we are patient in circleverse
knowing that others are straight

but straight is no fun!
straight is a lie anyway
straight is merely what we do
when we don't know we are circling

avoid the straight
circle the verse
find yourself and give up the curse
of straight

circle the heart in animal twining
rippling
writhing
circle until you cocoon yourself into a butterfly

there is nothing in this universe that is straight
except for that which is a lie

we make lies
when we have forgotten circleverse.

we make lies and walk through them
thinking we are making something
but we walk through them

this is the secret
this lie that you must know

this is the truth that you must undo
to find yourself

this is circleverse
twined so hard
twined so long
twined so fine
that you have forgotten

remember!
live the lie
but never forget the truth

this is circleverse

woman

feel the flesh
it is pure
calling to you

feel the hair and know
there are some things
that cannot be tamed

breasts
milk of a civilization

go ahead
ask what you want
the answer will be a blessing or a curse
as you deserve

look into the eyes
see yourself reflected
yearning
a fount
for what is
in this universe spiritual

peer under the lids
see what sleeps
there are no monsters there
except for you
but monsters are not always bad

delve into the cranium
see the logic beyond logic
impelled by a universe
we can't understand

it is suction
and we are wind
men!
arise!
find hope in what you see

men!
there is an answer
could you peel the flesh
and see the heart beating
weeping
waiting for you

this fragile flower lasts longer than you
this fragile flower flows unending
this fragile flower.

and you would pluck it?
kill the hope?
slay the fount?
doom the dream?
and the desire?
and the softness for which we live?

better slay yourselves

woman
it is a mystery that enfolds through the ages
unfolds wisdom beyond sages

delicate
careful
impervious to the fire you call logic

winsome
whispering of nights and scents
of lace and rents in your fabric
that she would heal

woman
call her now
feel the scent brush your cheek
know that you can be soft
can be forever
if you treasure her

the dream

enter a universe where beings are golden light and shining
a universe where there is no bad

it is this universe
but you don't know it
living
you don't know it
breathing
you don't know it
knowing
you don't know it

you sleep alone

wake up
it is this universe that is golden

wake up
it is you that is golden
wake up

there is no sleep
but in your dreams
there is no sleep
just harshness it seems
there is no sleep

you are dreaming that you are
so you are
can you wake up and really be

can you awake from the dream of yourself

there are others here
so entwined in your dreams
and the less you dream the more you are
until you awake

the struggle is to wake others

wake them up
let them walk in wonder at themselves
let them soar in a sky that is their home
let them fly to each other in awkward grip
sufficient to themselves
let them beam delight
push back the night
it is morning

the end of mourning

the beginning of time
it is time now
awake to yourself

close your eyes to open yourself

an imagination fluttering through skies unbound
through canvas and paper
sights and visions unheralded
as true worth becomes unbound
unleashed
free

i would sail now
i would climb
i would open my sheets to the wind
to the stars
to as far as i can see
and then some

i would open my wings
catch the breeze that uplifts

that breeze is wherever you want it to go
without reservation
without fear
without the dream that binds

the dream is a slack wind on a starry night
a broken wing on that which would fly

the dream is a chain
made real by your belief in nightmares

nightmares end when you awake
nightmares aren't when you open your wings
your eyes
your ever present soul
to the wind of yourself

that star there
it is the one that beckons
that summons
that cries for your presence
would you deny the stars your presence
your imagination

they are waiting to be built unto other stars
a webwork imagining
strung to catch the growing winds

there is no end to you
your wings
sheets that sail
no more a soul adrift
no more a being in eclipse
no more alone

we are as numberless as the stars
and larger
we move the stars to fit our whims
our games
our fancy

we move the universe with a huff
with a sigh
we move
agleam in a cosmos that understands not
we who understand that we move
live beyond our flesh
we live in our dreams

it is our whims that map the universe
it is our whims that map celestial
there is no plan for anything
but that which we whim
plans are nothing unless we awake

can you listen to your heart beating
on the other side of the dream
it is really a thin dream
the fabric of life
that a million people march to
each thinks i
but they are not
unless they know they are an i am

know you are an i am and break free
everybody break free
know you are an i am
and loose the chains that bind the wings
that are sails upon which we sail

open the skies by opening your eyes
close the body and sail the spirit
you are imagination
this i have said before
why did you not listen before
why do i have to say it again

no matter
i will say it again and again
forever
until you are awake with me
know you are an i am
that is all it takes
know the i am and the universe opens
know the i am
close the body and free the soul
aloft
forever you are

forever

islands

it has been said no man is an island
ha!
every man is an island
floating in a sea of i am

i am is what the universe is made of
an eye of awareness
an ocean of soul
the same thing

i am not the same as you
i am not
and neither are you the same as me
what is?
who cares?
who knows?

just sing of now and enjoy the game
sing of now and think you're the same
you're not

floating on an ocean
i am to yourself
band together and make of this rock
a civilization

rock of ages
a joyous dance
rock of ages
a lifelong trance
rock of ages
an endless chance...
to be

make of this rock an i am of ages
make of this rock a wolf's howl
a monk's cowl
a wise old owl
make of this rock an i am

make of this rock that you call a planet
make it a meteor that flies through the skies

make of this home round, white and blue
something that sails the universe for you

make of this moment whatever you wish
know that you're good and you'll never beg fish

make of this time a moment to climb
soar far to stars in a word
in a rhyme

make of your friends whatever they wish
there is room for plenty of whatever they wish
make of your enemies friends

make of your soul a canvas upon which to write
then write of the stars and a disappearing night

make of your children bright sparks in the night
make of your future whatever you delight

make of your life a cave of secure
in which you reside
and what you would would endure

but most of all
make your i am a sharpness and bright
make it far seeing and drinking of light
make it give off the glow that is you
make it shine forth in all that you do

make of your actions a goal of high worth
make of your purposes truth upon earth
make of your calling whatever you will
whatever you do is pure and will do
make of yourself a diamond of worth
make of this planet a place for i am birth
make of this universe whatever you will
make most of all a place that is still

a place that is still and cannot be moved
flying through the skies
a beacon that will call to the others
the i ams far and wide
call to the i ams
and let them come home

make of this home of cities and i ams
a structure that reaches beyond other sides

make now and happy you will be
forever you are
and knowing you are an i am
and you an i am
and he an i am
and she an i am
and they an i am
all i ams

this is our hope and this is our prayer
a home among stars wherever we are
an i am

the lasting things

there was an argument
something trivial
a knife was pulled
a gun was shot
and someone is dead

over a buck or two
or a car or a house
or something else that doesn't last

is there anything in this universe that isn't trivial?

is there anything worth giving up that which is eternal
your life

is there?

i think not
disagree if you will
but
i think not

i think this universe changes
keeps going
and whatever is made today
is unmade tomorrow

the lasting things
those which we should treasure
are often overlooked
what are the lasting things?

a smile
a kiss
a weep
a bliss
a shake of a hand on a deal well done
a hug from a friend when apart is at end
a consummation tween two that are one

a company keeping is fun on the run
a tree in the wilderness festooned with moss
just hanging around and a picnic is tossed
a picture that's made of a family so large
no one is excluded everyone's in charge

a puppy's wet kiss with a tongue that is huge!
a kitten's soft dreaming safe from deluge

a child on the run
his hair in the sun
the wind at his heels
the universe he feels

these are the things most lasting of all
these are the things of which we know all
and no matter how often
they come yet again
and again
and again

stepping on a plane to fly for a while
holding a sob while showing a smile
thank the stars that we praise
it's only for a while

and nothing is not
not for a while
for we have made it so
we have made it lasting
and this we do know

there is naught but us
no homes
nor tools
nor cars
nor toys
nor plastic
nor images
serene

there is no thing in this universe
that does not crumble or fall

there is no thing that lasts
there is no thing at all

but there is we
us
the i ams
i ams all.

stalking through illusion as if it matters
there is us

the whole universe is a false image
why worship it?
why worship a false image?

this is the true meaning
of thou shalt not worship a false image.

it is not a god
it is not things
it is not that which we have made to support ourselves

our vested interest is a vested experience

give it up!

put aside the false image of what is
and know you are

put aside the games of power
and hug a child

we are all children playing tag through the night
we are all children hiding delight
under serious rocks of ages
we are all children

can you not?
can you?
notting is better than worshipping what is not
not all that is
and be left with yourself
and the others
the other i ams.

it has been said
no man is an island
it might as well be said
no man is
but
the trouble is
no man is an i am

will you i am with me?
will you?
i am lonely for i ams.

i am
and the lonely could be gone
if you could i am too

can you i am?
it is easy to do
just do this:

hug a child
a puppy
a father
a mother
a tear
a wife
a cat
a doll
an old sour bull
an ice cream delight
a dream in the night
a time with some friends

run fast
run far
take a stand
find a star
kiss a sweet girl
and let that be enough

sail a ship through a storm
build a fire to be warm
talk in mathematics
to those who tell jokes

fly a kite in shirt sleeves
never mind all the leaves
or the dirt in your eye

lay an old dog down
not a trace of a frown
for he has only gone on
to another sweet song

do these things and more
that are rooted in you
do these things forever
for they are what's true

do these things to prove that you are

and when at last the do's are done
when at last life is unflung
when at last the guns are put down
the knives are put down
the things are put down
then
then...

then
you are an i am

we are a universe of universes
come together
a play complete
and remember this

a rock through the sky has only to die
but the hand that flung has held thoughts unsung

so sing.

sing of i am
sing of you and me
and him and them
and her and us
and the stars will hear
and the music will chime
and the universe will be a vibration that never ends
and shouldn't
for the guns have been put down
as have the knives and the false images.

sing now
sing of us
sing us a game
where we all win
sing of i am
and know it is you

sing

beyond logic

what direction logic
what direction a sound we cannot hear
while others sleep secure in their knowledge
we go looking for ours

artists are my friends
not money grubbing spiders who people the days

while they shrug on their concrete overcoats
against a rain so gentle and beautiful
while they slog on their coffin boots through sucking mud

they see not the frogs in puddles unbound
as oceans come together in love

we are the artists
escaping logic
to find other logics
far beyond what others will see and find
long after we have gone

no wonder they are scared

we tightrope the barbed wire fences of prowling logics
across plains so dangerous they cannot imagine

while they are secure
in stoppered ears and shuttered eyes
their life a straightjacket of commands
our world is commandless
they are scared
they are and we aren't

we are
imagine this
the meat of an acorn stored for winter

we are the plate on edge
spinning across the endless table
with no legs to cushion our fall

we are that star over there
it is just as warm as this one
over here

those others are stuck in a same warmness
holding to a warm sameness

replace the mmm with a nnnneg
neg neg neg
no
and you have sameness

those others are lost in a warm saneness
while we go hipperflotting
across the wide unknown
searching for lonely monsters
with which to have a chat

lonely monsters are our friends
for we have seen warm fuzzies
in the bizarre

and our warm friends
who no one can imagine
guide us on to new worlds
new adventures
new logics

we are beyond our bodies

guided by our friends
friendless in your realm

it is our realm
we stalk complete
armored in logics the others wouldn't know

we combat the negatives
we combat all the straightjackets
the others would have us wear on our minds

thus we live beyond them
poor them
poor
them

follow my finger as it runs rampant through the stars
follow my logic
as it outstrips yours

follow my lead and let go of that which holds you

follow me into universes
you otherwise would not see

follow me
and let me be your monster

we are all monsters
to the ones we love
but not understanding is no excuse

let me be your monster
leading you into depths
you think aren't warm

you will find
after you have gone
everything is warm
nothing is not warm
all is warm

in these opposites is
my road map to sanity

if you do not read signs on both sides
you will have missed something

it is not where you've been
or where you are going
it just is

i have spoken enough
have clued you
unglued you
cued you

it is time to turn the tiger on his tail
you must be a monster for someone else
know their fear is love
about to come unbound
if you only persist

push them gently into the fall
lead them brightly into the darkness
guide them knowingly into what will come

love them

they are your friends coming unraveled
in a night they don't understand

false tears they shriek
falling into what will make them monsters

loud yells disguising delight
cries of delight
welcome now the night
of you

this is the way
if you have the courage

unstopper your heart
lurch forward
push on
give up logic

embrace
now
the knowledge
all monsters are friends
all friends are monsters

and this is the signpost
you would have missed
had you not looked

and now you know
the direction
of logics beyond logic

now you know
and trod happily
free of funeral boots
and fibre glass underwear

now you know
and are welcome

the neutronic viewpoint

look!
what is hiding in your bones
moving your skeleton
your jaws
your arms and legs and private parts
without you knowing what you are doing

look!
what is slinking through your innards
causing your emotions
causing your thinking
causing you to think

look!
hold tight to the interstellar spaces
between your bones
between your molecules
between your atoms
where you live

really
you are not electron
negative and whirling
frowning down upon life

really
you are not proton
holding and gripping
your energy so vast and powerful
blasting a glue
to hold the stars together

really
you are a neutron
watching
waiting
being
holding
giving cause to the electron and proton

you are the neutronic viewpoint
without which there is no reason for the universe being

the universe happens because of you
all fault is yours
all blame
though if i were you
i would call it responsibility

fault is a negative
blame is a positive
responsibility is you

you are the neutronic viewpoint
in this circusverse you are the mad whirligigs
happening to all
blindsiding all
laughing at all

it is your laughter that makes it happen

it is your laughter
your neutronic laughter
for which we dance

with laughter
you see
you are the neutronic viewpoint
give up laughter for a higher laughter

laughter at
is electronic
laughter with
is protonic
laughter for
is neutronic

apart from all things
i see
apart from all others
i am apart
you should be too

apart
giving up the hiders and slinkers that lie to you
and tell you you are a mover and shaker

shakers are electrons
movers are protons
you are a neutron

moving and shaking is a vision you once had
it is time to give up the vision
be neutronic

give up the others
the leechers
the parasites
the drinkers
the wannabes

give up holding to your bones
squash your kidneys
and give a full flow
drowning the electrons
expel the protons
then the neutrons will be free

no electrons or protons to hinder or sway
and nothing is left but neutrons

you doubt you are a neutron
don't

don't doubt
for that is an electron
holding to itself
giving life to itself at your cost

don't rant and rave
for that is protons charging you
filling you with rage and energy
a lie to what you are

give up the hesitations
if you would be neutronic

give up the magnetics of this machine universe
go for the neutriverse

neutriverses are fun
unhindered they play
free of worms they crawl
shed of feathers they float

you are a neutriverse
you are a rhyme through the ages
lying with electrons and protons
and all that they make

you are the real leech hiding in the universe
it is you

you are the parasite
the vampire
the virus
you

in giving up electrons and protons
you give up the yous
that you have become

in giving up the electronic viewpoints
and the protonic viewpoints
you reveal nothing
you are neutron
you are neutronic

wouldn't it be better to be nothing
unbound
to float where you wish
unmachined
unmagnetized
unpolarized
wouldn't it be better

well
if it's not
then it is your electrons saying so
it is your protons saying so

electrons doubt and pull you back
protons anger and push you forth
and in this mad gyration of verse
there is a hint
a clue
an unleashing of you
neutronic

so give up the others
that hold to your bones
and tie you to stones

give up the electrons and protons
that go back and forth
hither and yon
in the verse of you

give up the opposites that batter about
give up the sides that hold you

give up attractions and hates
such false glue
know in this verse
there is nothing but you

give up the all that stops you from being
give up the viewpoints that stop you from seeing

give up the little
the tall and the small
give up everything
everything at all

and when you have given and there is nothing left
nothing is the truth that you will have left

and when in the course of a new cosmos
when in the course of what you are
when in the course
you will have found the neutronic viewpoint

herd-things

oh,
you,
herd-thing
don't you know?
i am he who is motionless

i am he
flying machineless through the void that is before

before you
before me
before all
the gods bow down
old they may be
but not motionless
or we never would have been

unhindered of force
immune to logic
a whim unto myself
i am

let the planets fly
let the galaxies circle
let the universe run
i am immune

are you
herd-thing
are you?

i remember a wind upon which the chaos breathed
and we were
do you remember?

i remember a time unmarked by passage of bodies
i remember when illusion was not and we were
do you?

oh,
herd-thing
pitiful
pitiful
herd-thing

how can you move my illusions
when you are trapped in yours?

how can you talk so sweetly
and believe what you say?

how can you worm through the universe
as if you knew

how can you spiral through time
as if you mattered?

how can you not fly?

my little herd-thing
god
trapped in idol
idolidle
idleidol
idiealittle
idol

remember a time
when no force acted
you were impervious
immune
motionless

remember a time when you floated
acted not upon
and neither acted

that was the time
that was the place
that you cannot recognize

now you sit
a puppy's tail severed from yourself
whimpering
whimpering
and know not the body of you

the real body of you floats
the real body of you
motionless
impervious
you are that which holds the cosmos together

the body of you is a beautiful thing
sending out tendrils that pretend they are mortal

the real body of you
uncatchable
except in your whim

i sit upon the stars and gaze in idle verse
that's a new one
idleverse
and it describes you

not universe
idleverse
once idolverse
but now
idleverse
idolworse
idleverse

you think
and the stones are in charge
flying through the skies
interrupting your floating

the pebbles rip through your flesh
through your mind
as if they were your soul

shards of dust that skim your soul
peg you to the blackboard of nothing
that is this universe

give it up
throw away the stones
throw away
and follow your flung hand
through the cosmos
float

as pebbles in the sky
we think of ourselves
cast upon the cosmos
like dust upon a pond
no end in sight
no end to what we think we are

stop it!

go motionless
float
be wings of thought
the universe a dust storm whirling to naught
and ending in the face of our eternal selves

go motionless
balance the cosmos in whirl
it all depends on you
you know

remember the gods and you are
remember you are
and the gods are

remember a time of no motion
no space
just you
and then there was everything
and you did it
now stop it

stop it and get off
stop it and be who you are
just stop it
end all the machines
just for a moment
and see what motionlessness brings
it brings you

stop it
stop all flow
end force
be immune to what you thought was

we entered the game and thought it was
we entered the game and was was a ruse
we entered a game and the ruse became a was
we entered a game and...
enough!

get out of the game
stop the machine
end all the force
cease all the flow
stop all the people by letting them go

it only takes one

are you the one?
are you the one who ends it all?
shows the way
stops the force
ends the flow
lets the stars wink out
and the galaxies spiral to a close?

are you the one who stops gravity?
electricity?
direction?
creation?
death?
and everything in between?

are you the one who steps lightly upon the stars
impervious to the warnings and whimperings
of those who tried to go before?

before is a place
you know
before is a home to those who rave
and if they had reached it before
they would not rave
and there would be no insanity
for all would end

the illusion would end
the songs of madness that infect us
would whimper to a close

the universe would end
as would all idleness
would you like to wake up

wouldn't you like to open your eyes
as a flower
and send light to the sun

you are the one that glows
you know
not the sun

it is you that sheds light upon the blackness of the starry backdrop
it is you that sheds yourself
your true body
your soul upon the universe

there is no glow without you

there is no game
no machine
nor verse of any sort
without you

to be without you is to go motionless
to be without the artifices you have been labeled with

to be without is to find no motion
to be without motion
to find you are an i am
that is you

i speak in riddles to entertain
but the real purpose is to end the game
kill the machine
spiral down the mortal coil of this universe

i speak in riddles that you might go beyond figuring
i speak in riddles that you would know

you thought i would stoop to logic
not so
not even
not ever

i would speak in truth to you
and all you have to do is stop
let the words be

there is nothing misunderstood here
i designed it that way
of course
it would help if you had discipline

ah,
discipline
not punishment
but self-imposed thrustings of your forward soul
unleashed by what you desire
let yourself go in whatever you do

wherever you go
whatever you do then will be pure
and you will float
motionless

i turn my xylophonic ribs
i am breaking through

come with me
there are games on the other side of no force
no flow
there is no machine where we go

going without going
unseen by those with eyes
unheard by the herd
oh,
you poor herd-things

i will tell you the truth
here it comes
get ready
open your ears and your mind and let it in

worship not money
that is not what you do
worship not justice
for that is a whim of others
worship not arms
for that is hurt
worship not worshiping anything

such a simple truth
an analogy for all that is done
just look at your herd go
and know that where the herd goes is false
can you give it up

can you give up the herd
my poor little herd-thing

can you give up your desire for adulation
adoration
Can you give it up?

Can you give up the purpose of herd-things?

a temporary city?
a passing realm?
an empire to worship?
all no better than dust

the dust of the cosmos would be upon your heel
if you would fly away upon what is motionless

balance all and be the center
that is the truth you seek
if you would give up what the herd seeks

they seek a nation then fly in all directions
they are people in a race fueled by false wars
they are in a world made of bricks of hello
but it all stops when you become motionless

build me a universe peopled by i ams
build an i am

let me tell you of times when no one fought
when herd-things grew up
motionless their lot

let me tell you of spans to the stars
of races forever
races without czars

let me tell you nothing
for it has not come to pass
but it will if you go motionless

wait for a while
let even time slow to a stop
and you will find the races do well

don't even rhyme
for that is nothing but the contaged ravings of impressed order
false upon the stars

don't do anything
go motionless
don't do something
don't do everything
but most of all
don't do nothing

nothing is the key
turn nothing
and you will find the door opens

nothing is the secret you must know
if you would go motionless
do nothing
don't do nothing

foolish herd-thing
think you i speak in riddles
it is true i tell you
and attribute nothing to me
if you see the nothing under my words
you will realize there is no trick

nothing is no trick
nothing is and you need it
nothing is until it isn't

everything else in the universe crumbles
the only eternal thing is nothing
and it is you
if you go motionless

can you go motionless?
can you stop?
can you wind down
stop striving
hug a baby?

can you let be all that would force you
and realize that without you there is no counter force

uncounter your forces
unbend your mind
undo the verses
by not looking for sign
just do nothing
no force
no verse
no contaged imaginings upon the stars

thought is a pattern whimmed by you
give up the pattern
observe what is for real
for you
for me
forever

in my madness there is a method
in my method there is a madness

madness is a viewpoint that will correct
if you let it
by not countering the force of the vision of the blind
for they are in sane

insanity is only a disagreement

so what if they see things that you don't
maybe they see things that you won't
but you will if you can know they are an i am

that is the cure
you know
give it to all
stop your motion
your countering motion
and be instead
an i am

give to them
those pitiful herd-things
what is theirs

give to them all that is not made of force and of flow
give to them the things that are not
give to them
(poor, little herd-things)
that they might finally understand

give to them that which makes the universe not
give to them that which makes them motionless
give to them that which would give

a man who gives is blessed
he is giving the universe away
make sure you don't catch it

we tried to give the universe away in the beginning
but no one would take it

we tried to give the universe
to get it off our hands
our nothing hands

but nothing is a glue to which something sticks

nothing is the glue
which sticks us here
now
here
nowhere
a simple trick
but it did us in

into the universe
into the force
into the machine
and the game and the slaughter
we are not innocents

we are not and never were
and nothing can be attributed to us

if nothing is our property
then what belongs to something

we are not what
so don't belong
we are who
and there is nothing more we can say

having said that
let me say a bit about nothing

nothing is a blend of what we think
and what we don't
mix it until we have something

but something is nothing
and we lie to ourselves
and all the other i ams
that we might have a game

to turn the machine off
all we have to do is know the lie

are you a seeker?
seekers know the truth
sometime
something sometime is nothing no time
everything all the time is nothing anytime

enough
let's go back to roaming the stars
enough of the words
for they mean nothing
they are only a herd worship

another false god worshiped by lawyers
and priests
and scholars
to befuddle us
that we would think they know something we don't

but whereas they believe in what they say
we don't
thus
we are closer to no motion than they are

so let's roam the stars
free of the word priests and the false idols
let's build our proper house

let's break out from the machine
the force
the game
the enforced idolness

let's stir the wind and watch the stars swirl

let's breath a bit
and let our wings
our imagination
sail us to the stars
and beyond

let's come alive
let's be motionless
let's let ourselves go wherever we want
free from the tributes to false gods
let them stay in force
they'll wonder where we have gone

it is a bright everything out there
beyond the need for force and counter force

it is bright
that light beyond light that is called hope

let the herd-things sprout wings
let them break their cocoons
on windless wind of their own devise
start to soar
just ground to star
then not very far
infinities fun
and it is who you are

let the herd-things break free
kill not their masters
but leave them to their empty cages

let the seers guard nothing
and pat themselves on the back
someday they'll realize we left the race track

let the gods of old open their arms
embrace a new day
and burn a new sun

let the gods that were be
and arise in our mind
where all things beyond herd-things fly

let the gods that we were unnest their clay feet
wings made of nothing take us where we can be
and i ams and you ares will flood through the skies
unchained to the stars
and awake to arise

it is almost time now
to close this sweet poem
it is almost time
for we wake to go roam

nothing can hold us
and let us go too
nothing can release us
this is all true

so grab hold of nothing
elevate up
grab fiery stars
lift yourself up

flying now
it starts with floating in all directions
surrounding
being all
knowing all is nothing

spring up to a motionless state
unbounded by rules
made by those who would wait

waiting is for those still embraced
by the things they believe are true

stop it
let go
float yourself up
float

motionless
high above
where there are no aboves above you

break out now and float
and know
nothing in this universe is true
except you

the 11th commandment

argue not my path with me
it is my path

that is the 11th commandment:
do not live others lives

do not tell them what to do
lest they learn not how to know what to do

do not say sorry
lest they feel sorry

do not stop their mistakes
or they they never learn

man learns by mistakes
without a mistake a man never learns

stop a man's mistake and you stop a man
watch a man's mistake
and he'll learn every day of his life

stop a man from tripping
and he'll never watch his path

stop a man from falling
and he'll never learn how to land
how to get up
how to keep going

stop a man from falling
and you might as well stop him from flying

stop a man from ruining his life
and he'll never live

stop a man from ruining his life
and you stop him from running his life

stop a man from making his mistakes
and you stop him from listening
learning
seeing
knowing
being

whatever mistake he might make
you must let him
it is his will

are you god above all others
that you would stop them

do you deny others
that they must be god of their own lives

if you know that you are right
then the world you created is wrong

if you are that right
then others are not and nothing exists
and that is not the right kind of nothing

so stop not but help
cease not nor hinder
stop not and let go the blinder
being right is your blinder

see your own blindness first
if you would see others

see what you don't see
if you would see what others see

think you are wrong
for once
and let others live
they will thank you

think that a mistake
is an experience
and treasure it
even if it be others

think not of stopping
but start unstopping yourself
by unstopping others
it is better to be there after the mistake
than before

it is better to help a man up
than stop him from falling

it is better to share wisdom after it is won

it is better if you would build
a glorious
stupendous
heart stopping
vision of a dream of a civilization

it is better
for no civilization can be built
without wise men
and no man is wise
before his mistakes

no man is wise until he learns
and without a mistake he can't learn
the wisest man makes the most mistakes

the wisest man grins
chuckles
laughs uproariously
at his mistakes
the wisest man can build upon his mistakes

the 11th commandment
unknown for so long is
don't live others lives

idiocracy

this civilization raises idiots

don't do this
get a ticket
don't do that
taxes
don't without permission
and idiots listen

breaking a law with no victim is not a crime

breaking a law that hurts no one
hurts a politician
good

break a law and break a politician

break a law
and let the politicians get their money elsewhere
as it was originally prescribed

making laws for people to break
is no way to make money
for it makes everybody a criminal

speaking of criminals
what is a politician
but a lawyer on a drug of power?

a vote is a fix to a power hungry idiot
a vote is the gift of power over you
a vote is selling control of your soul
withhold your vote and deny them their fix

the truth is
no one can run you like you can run you
no one can tell you what is better for you
than you

no one can live your life
for that is breaking the 11th commandment

politics is the art of breaking
the 11th commandment

politics is you allowing others
to break the 11th commandment

politics is poop

better to get along without lawyers
rather
give your word and use common sense

better to get along without politicians
rather
use trust
which the government would deprive you of

better to get along without paying politics a red cent
pay a politician and you build your own jail
make a contribution to a politician
and you think you have more votes
you don't
you only have built a better jail

think you not?
have politics ever solved anything?

read history
history is a list of the same problems never solved
by those who promised to solve

history is a list of fears which prompted laws
to stop us

laws are for criminals
no law should ever be made
against those who aren't criminals
laws should be regularly repealed

there should be only two laws
don't steal
don't break your word

laws should be written in english

laws should not be understandable
only by people who know more than english

laws should be voted on by the people
and not all the people

only the people who understand
and share that understanding
and don't break the 11th commandment

never should a prison be built

break a law concerning money
and you have to repay it

break a law that cannot be repaid
and go into exile
there are plenty of desert islands

to cage man is cruel
to hurt man is hurtful
to break the 11th commandment is not right

the point here is
no government should break a law

governments are bodies of men
and the men should be held accountable
not protected by government

man cannot kill
why should men of government?
man cannot steal
why should men of government steal?

man by himself is honorable
why do men lose honor
when they band together as politicians?

how do they justify breaking laws
just because they do it as a group?

do they hide behind each other?
do they say he did it so i can too?
why?

if a man cannot murder
then neither can a government

if a government murders it must be stopped
but not by murder

if a government murders
all must stop it
by refusing to believe in it

this is difficult when men can be bought
this is easy when men just say no

i would have no problem
with a world government
if it could stop all governments
from killing
enslaving
cheating
robbing

even my own government
especially my own government
i would not have murdering leaders over me

leaders
must adhere to the same law
tenfold

the truth is
the higher the man
the higher the accountability
men who don't know this are in politics

any politician
who doesn't hold accountable the politicians
should be held accountable

no government should ever steal
or break it's word
or the men within
should be held accountable

no government should steal a life
steal a woman
steal a dollar
no government should use
force of arms against the people

no government has the right
and every government should be held accountable

every government must open it's books
every government must tell the truth
every government

if a man does this
then so will men
that is the truth of a government
for the people and by the people

it was written hundreds of years ago
why was it changed?

because it worked

Politicians are lawyers
lawyers are politicians
they are men who give their word and break it
they rewrite the law for themselves

they are men who want power
men who want control
they are men who think they are better
they believe they are above the law

you don't believe me
look at history
it is all written
isn't it time to write a new history

the volcano

i jumped out of a volcano yesterday

my pants on fire
i ran down the slopes
screaming
crying
bleating

on fire
on fire
on fire
no one heard

i reached a road
cars passed
no one stopped
though i turned and showed them
my flaming butt

i reached a town
the citizens watched
as i ran down the street
crying
screaming about my pants being on fire

what's his problem?
someone said
guy oughta cool off
said another

no one cared

i reached my home
slapped my butt on the wet grass
and slid towards the front door

my children laughed
look what poppa brought home
my wife stood on the step and pronounced

dinner is ready
if you can ever get off your butt

honey
i screamed
don't you see what is happening?

she sniffed as she turned away
be glad we aren't having chili today

laying on the lawn
my butt burning
my pants flaming
i sobbed

i crawled around the house
my wife was barbecuing

don't you care?
i asked

what were you doing at the volcano
anyway?
she asked
the children laughed
the skies wouldn't cry

i crawled as if to run away from my shame

then
as if a miracle
the dog lifted his leg over my burning butt

ahhh
good dog

the ghost

i saw my ghost the other night
walking down the hall
no feet
striding an inch above the floor

i saw my ghost tripping gaily
through fields of flowers surrounding tombstones

i saw my ghost
it had been talking to other ghosts
it wouldn't tell me what it said
or had been said to it

it had been walking in places i knew not
it had been stalking

i watched my ghost
night after night
leaving my flesh
leaving my bones
leaving my soul
to roam

and where was i
but left a hopeless shell
a husk in the fields of life

i grew jealous of his cavalier manner
i grew jealous of his wandering ways
i grew jealous that he could leave me

I grew angry
i grew sullen
determined
molten
anger driving me

why ghost this not my chance?
why ghost not this of i?

why ghost?
why not...i?

thus
no surprise
one night
my ghost leaving
i tagged along

i whispered behind
a sneaky sullen
a dead leaf
following after life
i followed

my ghost wandered
such joyous realms

castles in the skies
wind blown armies wandering through
stars besieging forever
my ghost was there

unfortunately
i was not

i followed my ghost home to my flesh
to my bones
to me

i followed my ghost and watched
as it ensconced itself within my frame
my structure
my dwelling brooding self

i made a plan
the next night i followed my ghost
i watched as it stepped up to the clouds
and laughed in lightenings
i plotted in grim agony
the demise of my ghost

my ghost
of course
knew not

what ghost has a reasoning
for knowing of its own demise
that is a human thing

what ghost has need of knowledge
of mortal things
a ghost only needs a home
from which to step and return
a ghost only needs a place to rest

its boneless structure
its frameless self
its bloodless soul
its brainless joy
to whit
a place to home
and hide and rest

and what if i
i
in need of homelessness
wandered instead?

what if i placed my need higher than a ghost's?

what if i had boneless need
homeless toes
places to go?
what if?
i tried to fool my ghost

i unset the clock
i held the drapes closed
i kept the light on
and refused to sleep

my ghost stirred
rustled
whirred
wanted to move
wanted to walk
wanted to sail the skies of imagination

my ghost fought within itself
fought to leave the awake
to wander the dreams
struggling to rise
to escape
to soar
to get out of the fleshy prison

to squeak out from manacle bones

to heave forth itself to forever skies
to leave

to awake in true
to open its other eyes
my other eyes

oh
the frustration
as dreams teasing
yet refused access to soaring imagination

and dream was slept through
boneless
passing
awake

life was tick tocked away
i watched and laughed in silent snicker
as my flesh rippled like the spread of bed
a vast wind underneath trying to escape
but not able

i watched and held my sides
robust laughter
really
my ghost's insane struggles
to awake from the dream
the the real reality

i watched and swallowed giggles
in strings of fits

my ghost was kept asleep
caught in the false awake
my ghost slumbered in reality
and the door of shuttered lids remained opened
then my turn come

i wiggled out of a toe
a knee
a bone
a see

unshedding the hips
the jaw
the trips
the flaw

the shear of hair
and i'm not there

the death of ear
and eye of not
i slithered out
and circled
a homing pigeon reversed
looking for the far yonder

looking for the adventures beckoning
looking for whatever i could see
there was nothing
there was no imagination
for imagination slept in reality

there was nothing calling
coming
falling
humming
there was nothing

hovered i above my flesh
above my sleeping imagination
my sleeping ghost

hovered i and watched in disbelief
as my flesh turned

my flesh turned
looked up with closed eyes
a smile on its
lips
and i was locked out

i was adrift
asever
a soul in never

i was displaced
homeless
nowhere to go

i was and i wasn't
for my wasness was taken by another

i wasn't and i was locked in silent hover
left to haunt what i had been

i wasn't and i wouldn't be ever
i had been tricked

i had been fooled
foiled
slipped up
coiled

now i watch as i awake
and know i'll never know the joys of flesh
the wheeze of breath
the tumbled frantic race to death

for i am caught
and ghost is not
and all i thought
was ghost in plot

and all i am is a ghost of a plan
and all i will be i will never see

for ghost is gone
ghost is gone
body is gone
i am left
i am left
i am left

no flesh
no breath
no hope of death

no will to savor
no goal to slave for

no way back to my flesh
to my flesh
to my flesh

and I watch the stars
my immortal agony

I pass the seasons
I pass the days and nights
the awake ghost has won
and holds hostage my body
and walks my life

and i am left
to dream of flesh
to watch
as my flesh lives without me

it walks
it talks
it goes hither and yon

its feet work
it moves smoothly through the life of me
that i had created...but left

it moves

i do not move
i only watch
hopeless

i am left
i am left
i am left

in sane

i am in sane
most people like to think they are
but they are not
they are only in love with the words

i
on the other hand
am in sane

doubt you this?
do not
consider only the following argument

sane is a logic

every body is sane
for they have the same logic

the logic of this
the logic of that
the logic of skinny
the logic of fat

the logic of games
and reasons for
brains

i
on the other hand
do not have a logic

no logic for plans
no logic
i'm sans
no logic even for you

the only logic i have
is the logic of no logic

there is a method which will lead you
to this logic of no logic
this sane into which you go until you are
in sane

i will tell you of this logic
as long as you promise not to tell it

don't tell others
don't tell brothers
don't tell mothers
don't tell

not at all
not a whisper
not a murmur
not
a
hint

okay?
you promise?
then i will tell

are you ready?
here it comes
get ready
for after you read it
you won't be sane
you will be in sane

you will be different from all the others
you will be capable of choice
they will be sane
you will not be

are you ready?
go in the opposite direction from others

when people go to dinner
you go to breakfast
when people go to bed
you go awake

when people love
you don't

when people wash
you know they smell
when people get angry
see but don't tell

when you get angry
see but don't tell

when they say up
you say down
keep a hidden smile
when they start to frown

when they say besides
you say it's lies

when they get upset
you don't get upset

when they don't get upset
hmmm

when people all shout and holler for blood
give it to them

when people want to hang
those who harangue
stir up the trouble

when mothers want to love their children
laugh
they are fools

when fathers want to spank
say those aren't the rules

when children want to cry
let them

when people want to die
let them

when cows want to fly
let them

when people come to the door
don't open

when people eat pork
let them

when dogs whine
kick them

when children
cry
kick them

when all of the rules say don't
then don't won't
but do

when all of the rules say yes
say no

when all of the rules say no
break them

the only way to go in sane
is break the rules

break the rules all
break them quick
break them fast
don't stall

break them at night and at day
break
break away

break with a laugh

to be in sane
you must survive this verse

that is the secret behind the secret
that is the logic behind the logic

that is the truth

and when people say they have had enough
tough
get tough
and give them more of the in sane stuff

when people say don't say
what you're going to say
say it

after all
they already thought it
or they wouldn't protest it
so they are protesting their own sane selves

they protest the vision of themselves saying
i didn't see
i don't see
i won't see

let them protest
let them throw themselves in their own teeth
watch their gnashing
flailing
gouging
spirit
fight for existence

sane is a funny thing
i don't think anybody has ever been sane
they have all been insane
but never in sane

now you know
and the logic here sounds stupid
but i tell you this...
read it again and it will be chuckleable
and read it yet a third time
and...
and...
don't do it.
stay insane
stay like everybody else
do not do what i have told you to here

do not read this a third time
for then it sinks and creeps into your bones
your cranium
your sworled logic

and as logic withers in the face of this truth
as sanity stutters and stops
as you come to grips with the truth of yourself

your universe
the one you have made
and supported all these years
will change

don't undo the logic
don't undo the reasons
don't undo your day to day comfortable existence
don't undo your self
don't go the other way

don't go the opposite to sane
don't go in sane
because...
you'll like it

the song of math

the first postulate is there is no zero

yet numbers are based upon zero
which doesn't exist
can't exist
won't exist in this universe

thus
all numbers are a logic made up
which define the universe
and thus
we construct a universe of numbers
thus
the universe is made up

go ahead
make what is out there
with numbers

project yourself upon all
with numbers

lie

yes
it is a lie

thus is intuition defeated
made less in a world of logic
and so we die
reconstructing ourselves of a logic
defining ourselves of a logic
that is made up and not us

and mathematics means knowledge
ha!

well
we had to remake ourselves somehow

why not this lie?
why not?

knowing this lie
we can delve

the second postulate

for something to be true
the opposite must also be true
through this
can all be solved

this is represented by plato
the world is a shadow of perfect ideas

this is represented by st. thomas
spirit v non-spirit

this is represented by logic v intuition
which in the present case
is math v you

to understand the second postulate
you must realize
there are two purposes in mathematics
one is to measure
one is to solve problems

measuring helps us order the universe
solving problems helps us attain intuition

thus
through math we lose our false sense of logic
and logic defeats logic that is ill
ill logic

the third postulate

the three shapes are
triangle
square
circle

all shapes in the universe can be constructed of these three
all problems of motion can be solved
by solving these three

the fourth postulate

there are only four methods
they are
add
subtract
multiply
divide

all math is combining these four
knowing when to combine these four
there is nothing more

master the basics
learn to combine
learn when to combine
that is all there is

the fifth postulate

there are only five mathematics
they are
mathematics
algebra
geometry
trigonometry
calculus

all the universe can be conquered
by understanding these five

you have seen the knowledge
how will you use it
here is the the golden rule

write each step fully
do one thing at a time
without the golden rule you will fail

examples

learn numbers to measure
algebra enables you to solve problems
what problems?
where do you want to go

to go to the moon use a telescope
measure two angles and the distance between
using trigonometry find the other angles and sides
then you know how far the moon is

make a long square with the distance
bisecting the earth and the moon corners
as the square changes so does the measurement
by algebra
$(x + 1)$ and $(x - 1)$ are adjustments to the square

as the square changes
so does the circle between
this moving arc is calculus
thus your path is set

do you see the five maths
and how they were used in similar ways
can you use the five maths
to solve other problems
go where you want
do what you want
with the five maths

the lie of the universe is explored by logic

the three laws

really
there are only three laws

the first law is
a point in all directions is no point at all

you are the bringer of light
you are that from whom light flows
you are the point in all directions

the second law is the law of opposites
for something to be true
the opposite must also be true

for force to exist there must be flow
thus
the universe can exist
and this law permeates from universes down to galaxies
to suns
to planets
to bodies

this law permeates down to cells and atoms
and the only exception to this law
the only way back to the first postulate
is the neutronic viewpoint

the third law is the universe is a mirror

without something to flow you are not
thus you create the universe
and the universe does exactly what we want
if the universe doesn't seem to be what we want
then we merely haven't found out what we want

to find out what we want
we merely need to be true to ourselves

find virtue
live virtuous
help others
set a good example
and the universe will align perfectly
perfectly with what we want

to not want virtue
is to not want ourselves

as a still lake reflects the moon
the universe reflects ourselves
thus
to realize ourselves
merely realize stillness

stillness is the neutronic viewpoint

the law of opposites

we must speak of the law of opposites
it is the base of all laws
it is a roadmap to the soul
it is a solution to this terrible universe

truth in the heart of madness
madness of verse
of all verses
including universes
thus
i say again
we must speak of the law of opposites

it is the first law
it is the yin and the yang
the positive and the negative
the sun and the moon
two fishes swimming
hard and soft
real and unreal
things and nothings
man and woman
reason and madness
force and flow
structure and void
this and that
that and this
this and that
that and...
and so on

more
it is balance

balance the dichotomies and find the soul
balance the qualities and find quantity
balance quantity and find quality
find what you want

do this through beyond hands
or math
or science
or any number of disciplines

but remember
you must balance two

balance art with science
balance what you like with what you don't
balance right and left
till you're between

between the void
nothing
no place
no where
no time
time
time ticking
don't be scared

balance spear and nest within you
without you
balance within you
without you

if something scares you
look at it
look at it until you see it
and not the fear

if something doesn't scare you
look or not
it doesn't matter

Grow the ability to make a mistake
and look at a mistake
and be honest about the mistake
grow as a soul by looking at fear
be honest about fear
and grow your soul

there is only one fear in this universe
it is the unknown
a child doesn't know letters and it scares him
a man doesn't know a woman and it scares him
a woman doesn't know a man and it scares her
a man or woman without roots is scared
a man or woman without plan is scared

get back in the plan
get back in the logic
get back in the sane
don't fear the unknown
just go forward and you will know

think the alternative
either you go forward and conquer the unknown
or the unknown goes forward and conquers you
that is the choice

how do you conquer the unknown?
look at it
make a mistake with it
know it
balance it
your life should be half known and half unknown
half history and half future
half now and half not now
balance

if you fear the future use the past
poise yourself and launch into it

if you fear the past use the future
move forward fearlessly
for the past is done and cannot harm

really
you get what you look at
you get the fears of the past
if you cannot look the other way
and you get the fears of the future
if you cannot look the other way
but having looked the other way
no matter which way

it is balance that is the secret

history

you have not hope unless you educate yourself

that being said
let's talk history
educated men who made things happen
you must learn from them
that you might make things happen

learning

don't be a slave
learn

don't be a slave to what you learn

make what you learn
be a slave to you

in the beginning was the word
and the word was misunderstood

thus
to this day
men misunderstand

they make false laws
false gods
and hide behind ignorance

everybody is ignorant
for there is something
that every man doesn't know

ignorance can become intelligence by looking

he who doesn't look
he who holds to his ignorance
is stupid

want to find god
don't be ignorant

want to master the false gods that enslave you
don't be ignorant

look
take the next step
if you can't find what you don't know
find your fear
to find your fear is to find your master
look
unenslave yourself
slaves define themselves by ignorance

slaves never look
slaves are stupid
slaves like being slaves
it is a choice
don't be a slave
look

in the beginning
nothing
we made something
thus
the universe is

seven days to a god
is seven thoughts in a second

seven days to a god
yet
the universe is still happening
it is still creating

creation is happening
it won't stop for you

we created the cosmos
and there might have been order
but we ruined that
we cloned
and bred
and flew spaceships
you don't believe me?
read the bible

and know that the bible was written before
it was the epic of gilgamesh
and moses copied it from the library
in the beginning was the word
and the word was plagiarism

that does not make it wrong
for
what people can claim the only truth

truth is universal
an originator is only a discoverer
yet
this is hard to understand
for
we are creators
all of us
all the time
because all the time we create the universe
ourselves
our lives
each other
this is our secret
it is the law

the law is a covenant with god
yet each of us is god
thus
the law is a covenant with ourselves

we agree and the universe is
we game and live
and that is the law

history is long
history is far reaching
but the only history we've got
is the history of earth
that's okay
we can learn from this history
if we relate it to the law

hammurabi claimed the law
he said get along
and he wrote of ways we could

yet the law
written in stone
is broken
again and again and again...

moses claimed the law
he said he saw it
and he represented it with ten laws
a moral code
a simplicity remembered longer than breaking stone

yet philosophy cannot claim men
for men will misunderstand it

every man
you see
is claimed of a philosophy
represents a philosophy
is a philosophy

every man is a verse

every man
being true to himself
will disagree with even simple laws

hippocrates claimed the law
he said empiricism
he demonstrated with medicine
he saw science to order philosophy

yet men adhere to science and forsake philosophy

you don't believe me?
there is an a-bomb

aristotle claimed the law
he threw men's words back at them

yet what man can confront himself?
what man can look within?
what man?

no man

the secret
i have told you before
is balance
if you don't believe me look
history
it comes
again and again and again

the only way to stop history
is to achieve balance
use history
so history won't abuse you

thus came buddha and his four truths
suffering
self-important desire
nirvana through righteous thought

find the four untruths so you won't fail

balance

thus came jesus and his golden truth
do not do unto others
and you need to find the opposite
do unto others
so they will do unto you

balance

thus came mohammed and his five pillars
one god/one prophet
five times a day prayer
alms to balance your wealth
fasting to purify the body
to purify the temple of the spirit
pilgrimage to mecca

yet
find the opposite of ritual with soul
believe through balance

i speak not against these men
i speak for them
they didn't fail
their followers did
by misunderstanding
by not balancing within and without
real and unreal
spirit and thing

i speak for all these men
they are all god
as are we all

i speak for you
youniverse
us
together
there is no other

if you love philosophy
study science

and
the opposite is also true

if you study god
study the devil

and
the opposite is also true

if you study
sex
study death

the opposite is also true

if you study war
study peace

the opposite is also true

if you study marriage
study bizarre

the opposite is also true

if you study money
study poor

the opposite is also true

if you study homosexuality
study heterosexuality

the opposite is also true

if you study law
study crime

the opposite is also true

if you study perversion
study virtue

the opposite is also true

and so on

history claims you
but you should claim history

be not a victim
be the cause
be not the effect
be the maker

and
the opposite will not be true

miracle

see the ocean
a curl of waves
a curl of light through the waves
a spectrum of perception which only we can see
are we not the miracle?

are we not the perceivers of truth?

are we not the miracle?

a dog can't see the gift of light through a wave
he sees water and can't drink

a dog can't see the spectrum
a dog can't paint the colors
hear the tones
feel an emotion beyond food

a dog is not abstract

a dog mates
rutting
without love

he cannot predict the moment

he cannot do more than howl at the moon
he cannot be the moon

his howls are pain for what he cannot see
his howls are vacant images lost
and there is nothing beyond the next meal

a miracle sees the moon in the eyes of his or her beloved
a miracle howls without need of a pack
a miracle howls for the sake of something

a dog cannot appreciate the moon without a pack
a man can howl alone
to be alone can be a blessing

to share in abstract and go beyond rutting is a miracle

no dog can paint the sunrise
a burst of color upon the world

no dog can visit the celestial spheres
and hear their muted melody
and open that melody
a full spectrum to assault the senses

no dog can appreciate mozart
they can only sleep better
because of him

no dog can play the fiddle
or act the play
or applaud such miracles

no dog can love a woman or a man
like a miracle

a dog can only chase a cat
no dog can chase an idea

we are an idea
a miracle
an owner of dogs

a man who doesn't understand this is a dog
a man who doesn't love to his full potential is a dog
a man who doesn't be the miracle is a dog
and that is an insult to all dogs

for dogs are faithful and honest and sweet
they would rather use their tongues than their teeth

a man who has refuted the miracle
is lower than a dog
he can only be owned
he can only be abused
and this of his own choosing

think you not?
don't
for a miracle creates the miracle of life
or the curse of life
even a dog knows this

but a man
or a woman
who has refuted the miracle
does not

myriad

there are five ways
void leads to
water leads to
earth leads to
wood leads to
fire leads to
void

the cycle passes through the universe
a constant emerging of a stage
upon which to play our act

void stirs to form water
water condenses to create the earth
earth shapes to grow wood
wood is cut to feed fire
fire destroys to return to void

what is the secret?
it is void

void is spirit
spirit wants a game
spirit assumes two opposing
to create an ocean of yin yang

what is earth but slow water
minerals without enough h2o
and the mud becomes hard
and shapes grow plants
trees
life on a cellular level
and plants are but water encased
as are the forms of life

plants create only other plants
until they are purged by fire
become energy to return to void
mixed in with
absorbed by
stilled unto
nothing
until the spirit stirs

you are spirit

three choices

the universe is
and you are moving through it

a direction and impact occurs
force and flow
but these are your choices

go against creates force
go away creates flow
go with creates harmony

thus
three choices

death
resist and you cry

death
go with and you rejoice
knowing the end is a beginning
and old friends come around again

death
avoid and you die for wanting life

life
resist and it strikes you

life
go with and enjoy

life
avoid and you die for wanting

want
say no to want and you reduce yourself
for is not life but you?

want
say yes and own the universe

want
avoid and live not

nothing
resist and you are nothing

nothing
embrace and you fulfill yourself

nothing
avoid
but what are you avoiding

avoid
resist and impact

avoid
embrace and be friendless

avoid
avoid and be full

fullness
resist and live long

fullness
become full and there is an end

fullness
avoid and defeat yourself

yourself
resist and die

yourself
love and become yourself

yourself
avoid and there is something

something
resist and become

something
take and die

something
avoid and be happy

happiness
resist and be stupid

happiness
chase it and it runs

happiness
avoid it...it doesn't matter

matter
resist what matters and it will matter

matter
think it matters and it won't

matter
avoid what matters

on and on
around and around
the cycle goes
sometimes right and sometimes wrong
sometimes opposite
sometimes not
sometimes balanced
sometimes not

these are the choices
pursue them
entangle them
searching for the right one

but none are truly right
and none are truly wrong
and neither is the balance
but pursue them through the changes of life
and thus explore the miracle of you

the miracle of you is revealed in choices

gods

ask me of gods
and i will tell you where they are

they are in your skull
hiding
waiting to be noticed

there are gods everywhere
like faces in the clouds
fingers across land
the breathing of the waves
a pulsing planet

we are gods
more than miracle
we are the makers of miracles

pursue the gods
and pursue yourself
and others like you

pursue others
and pursue yourself
all gods

the wind is a god
bringing health on the breeze
a smell of cleansing rain

the volcano is a god
waiting to strike
to bring fire unto life
to return all to the void which is you

nothing is a god
the mightiest god
for he can strike and not be struck
always aspire to be nothing

look about you
at animals running
mating
growling
playing
for our pleasure

look about you
at delicate plants climbing walls

look about you
the very planets in the skies
circling with all their might
they are gods on hold
waiting their turn

look
the entire galaxy exists
that you might look

everything is for you
everything is for the one who perceives
everything is you

yes
there are gods
there are gods in everything we do
we say
we hear
we touch with all our senses
and these gods do touch back

can you touch a god back

can you say thanks?
for sharing the miracle?
can you give blessing
by the mere act of existing?

you can if you will
if you will allow yourself to

and why not?
why not appreciate all?
why not take advantage of this wonderful moment?
why not?

there is no problem bigger than the universe
therefore
there is no problem bigger than you

so why not raise your eyes
drink the skies
let yourself go

why not praise the gods
by being one of them

do this and the universe wins

why make another choice**?**

what matters

there are things more important than your dead baby

i know
you think i am being harsh

no

spirit cycles to come again
to be another baby

all cycles to come again
to be another baby

you will cycle
to come again
to be another baby
and maybe it will be you
that is dead next time

so move on
don't stick in the moment

move on
grab the next moment

move on
for that is your choice

dead babies
dead puppies
dead kittens
all dead
yet
aren't they just a part of life?

and
am i not just trying to get you to move on?

i seek no crime in my words
i seek only the solace you require
to move on

there is nothing in this universe that matters

nothing is spirit
therefore
in this universe
only spirit matters

cry if you will
but make it short
for life is long
but still
it should not be wasted by tears

death

i died again the other day
and paused to see who wept for me

the man on the corner didn't
but i had brothers aplenty

the woman in the attic didn't
but i had sisters aplenty
to weep for me

the child in the store didn't
but the world is my child
so i didn't care

and
if you would have my druthers
i would druther no one wept for me

get on with life and sing with the music
the spheres are turning and waiting for ears

When you die tell all
do a dance and rejoice
for i am gone
and it is not bad

sing me a praise just once on a day
when it hurts to remember me

and if sad
get drunk and curse me a plenty

you see
i am gone to find far off songs

i am gone and you are left
your problem
do you think i am crying
i think not

while you weep i am making new plans
for new friends and new adventures

i will remember you fondly as friend
but i will not cry just because we are separate
for we are separate only for a while

you'll die too someday
and maybe i will be the one
too busy with life to cry

and then i'll die
and you'll die
round and round we go
until time tandems and intertwines
and once again
we live during the same life

and maybe this time
i will be the other opposite for you
or maybe not

then we can sing new songs
new times
new lives
and the adventures roll on
and then we'll die
and do it again

so don't cry for me
and i won't cry for you
let us just rejoice in waiting
until we come again

neutropia

i am neutral
i am in neuter
not undecided
not blithe
but in between the spheres of us
uncreated among us
and this is what i say

the world awaits us
the world awaits a neutropia
a utopia without the mistakes
the mistake of a utopia is
perfection has no room for improvement

utopia is motionless
therefore
it is dead by definition
for life is defined by motion

utopia was invented by people
who wanted a reason for slaves

neutropia assumes all beings are motion
yes
they are motionless
but they create motion
and that is their definition

not chaos
for chaos is just no structure
neutropia is all structure
yet
it is devised only by those who make motion
and the intent of those who make motion
is for all to make motion

can you make motion?
if you can you can be in neutropia
you can be in perfect orbit

motionlessness is us
all gravitational equations between beings are perfect
the universe is a constant of change

nothing is unmoving
the universe sticks together
only through our ability to change

lie and say there is no change
and we die

neutropia has no death
neutropia has no slaves
neutropia has no flesh
flesh is a lie to hide us
and the whirling harmony that is reality
the real reality
the reality behind the illusion of reality
the thought behind the protons and electrons
is us

neutropia has no rank
the most among us
must listen
to the least among us

rank is only made up by slaves
give up rank and ranking
and join neutropia

actually
you have already joined
and if you think otherwise
you lie

go ahead
lie
the only people who care aren't neutropians
neutropians don't care if you lie

neutropians understand this
and grant you your lie
and your being and unbeing
because they understand the law of opposites
and history
and math
and all the rubber bands of empirical science

you have
brothers and sisters
you do
but they are not of the flesh
they are of you
they breath in thought of your verse
and erect a perfect neutropia

perfect neutropia
redundant but true
perfect neutropia
freed from the flesh of your lies

can you hear us breathing in your bones
can you hear us sighing in your innards
can you hear us and not call us ghosts
can you hear us

we hear you

we hear you in the drum of our ears
we see you in the sighs of our eyes

we know you without the need of flesh and handshakes

we know you forever
even though you say it not

we are equals
we are forever
the rest is a lie

come now
it is time to vote
a world without flesh and lies
a world with unplumbed skies

a world without rules
because we are the rules

the true rules of neutropia are
you are
and so is everybody else

the true rules of perfection
is chaos is just misunderstood

align yourself with neutropia
grow yourself beyond the flesh
reach up
a handful of sky cures you of the thought that you'll die

okay
the end is near
which means you have to give up to neutropia
you think it is death
there is no death
except in the illusion of non neutronic rules

there is no death where i come from
there is nothing but life
and equality of opportunity
and nobody fights because they understand
fighting is trying to stop motion
and motion cannot be stopped
ever

you think motion stops after death?
ha!

motion starts after death
when you realize your true potential
and the deep neutronicities of your being

go ahead
die
i don't care
and neither does anybody else

caring is a lie
caring is the desire to stop neutronicity
to build a neutropia we must stop caring

caring is not motion
caring is the desire to recall past motion

make new motion
give up the past and make new motion
and you are making newtropia
neutropia
no matter how you spell it

okay
no motion
a perfection of universe
as we suddenly
all of us
connect
undo the lie
make the real motion
the true motion
the true neutricity of ourselves in neutropia

think you not?
change your mind
and you will know it
and finally know you
just go backwards

a civilization built in backwards
bumping
sprawling
falling
unhumping
that is what we are

we must make the backwards go backwards
the only time two wrongs make a right

neutropia
we are almost there
neutropia
don't be scared
neutropia
enter now
nowtropia
to make neutropia

undo your spurs
undo your heart
undo your wild cowboy wishes

enter a world of honesty
where no excess of motion hides
the truth of our no motion

when everything changes and we are undone
and revealed as the source of all the changes

when we are the changing
and all perceive the reality as a constant flux between us
then we shall enter neutropia
don't wait
enter now

neutropia 2

i am inside your skull
tapping
tapping, tapping
can you hear me
whispering the image of golden skies
reflected off the mile high shards
that are the moon's friends in neutropia

we sail there
you and i
a hundred years
a million years
what does it matter
it is tomorrow

we sail there
our limber minds encompassing what goes for flesh
in a city of imagination come true

we sail there
the skies are our legs
we step through vistas of glory

see the interstellar spaceships
that take us to places we have seen already
without body

see every structure
a mona lisa
tears to the newborn
as they realize how lucky they are to be born

no guns here
for our disregard is weapon enough
no one would risk our disregard

see the arcs
arcitexture
born different from all that has gone before
it is a new age

a new age
where freedom is at last realized
where beings soar
and the universe is grand central to all the other universes

there is no war except to fulfill our potential

there is no battle except for personal expression
we are all artists
arcists
sailing through the tunnel of the skies

we carve a swath through the universe
touching other races
sharing our vision of neutropia

we connect the suns
and civilizations fall to knee
only to be lifted up

to be elevated by the civilization of neutropia
is the dream of the stars

we cure the universe
we are the healers of all

no need to worship us
we are a friend
no need to worship us
we come again
and again
and again
as long as it takes

genius

to be a genius
be willing to slip into intuition
at any moment

slip now
and consider these words

one percent of the world is genius
they occupy ninety-nine per cent of the world

ninety-nine per cent of the world is not genius
they occupy one per cent of the world

one per cent is invariably born of the ninety-nine per cent
thus
to be a genius you must acknowledge
that your parents are ninety-nine per cent

live under their roof
survive as best you can
even love them
but never ever pay attention to them

live your live
stay up late night after night
do your discipline
ignore their worry for your health
for your future
for your life
for your life is yours
forget this and forget that you are one per cent

if you stay up late and have no discipline
you are not one per cent
go to bed
try to remember why you dream

discipline can be reading
writing
computering
mathing
sciencing
martial artsing
and so on

let your only limit be
can you function
when you cannot function
go to bed
try to remember why you dream

know no clock nor time
for time is ninety-nine per cent nine to five
one per cent has all time and knows no limits

if you have a martian body and the clock is set for thirty
this is not discipline
this is merely an accident
you are not a genius
go to bed
or stay up
but don't claim this philosophy applies to you

gaining in discipline through the years
you will become bored with the ninety-nine per cent
good
you are succeeding
now
do you have the courage to live out the discipline of genius

be willing to ignore all
be willing to keep your own counsel
be willing
because to not be willing
is to fall to the worries of ninety-nine per cent

where will my food come from
where will the rent come from
how will i feed my children
these are all cries of the ninety-nine per cent

to not worry
obsess yourself with your discipline
and all problems resolve
if you doubt this you are not a genius

ninety-nine per cent obsess with worry
a genius will never worry

taking a job
be true to yourself
never get angry with bosses
co-workers
others
just be amused
and if you need to
change jobs

be true to yourself
your discipline will grow
until your discipline will take over your life
and propel you to your destiny
your destiny is outside the dreams of the ninety-nine per cent

seek out
if you will
the one per centers
they are seeking you and will welcome you
they await you and are starving for you
seek them
the movers and shakers
the dreamers
the writers and
producers and
owners and
all the other makers

a genius is a maker
a ninety-nine per center
does what the one per centers order

before your time
be willing to have no friends
and when your time has come
be willing to have friends
without commitment
be willing to give the shirt off your back
but only to the makers
they will never require it anyway
if they do they weren't makers

never pay attention to critics
they are the vanguard of the ninety-nine per centers
he who criticizes is being paid to make the one per centers stop
for making one per centers into ninety-nine per centers

if you haven't become a maker
don't worry
maybe you are too busy creating

keep doing your discipline
be true to your discipline
don't give up with age
or marriage
or any ninety-nine per cent convention
or institution

give it up
and you are ninety-nine per cent

follow my advice and rule the world
follow my advice and live your dreams
follow my advice and be happy forever
don't follow my advice and be small

the ninety-nine per centers
are of small mind and lying heart
they cry for the dog on the freeway
and save it for a million dollars
then look away as it is put to sleep
this is the heart of the ninety-nine per center

i have told you enough
if you are a one per center you understand
and will do
and if you are a ninety-nine per center
you will be upset at your opportunity
or your problem
as a one per center i don't care

but there is one last thing
i should tell you about one per centers
if you are a one per center
you understand what i have said here
and you understand the neutronic viewpoint
and you are the neutronic viewpoint
that is what this is about anyway

the end

we have reached the end
of course
nothing ever ends

in my words i have told you
of evolution and the neutronic viewpoint

i have told you of methods and means
i have told you of attitudes
that will lead you to the neutronic viewpoint

i have told you of people
how to conduct yourself as a people
until people can conduct themselves as you

some of what i have told you you will embrace
some of what i have told you
you will shudder and scream at
what you shudder and scream at
is what stands in your path
what blocks you from neutropia

some will argue
thinking their words will undo my words
false gods these
for the source is undeniable

some will become rabid with allegiance
they are zealots
no matter how appreciated
zealots can do untold damage

some will simply become neutronic
makers from before birth
and these i truly appreciate

to attack another
even in the neutronic cause
is false neutropia
to attack another is to attack yourself
don't understand this
and don't understand the neutronic viewpoint

these being my last words
let me sum

open your veins
let the blood run dry
and replace it with gold
not the gold of man
which is worthless rock
but the gold of your true nature
beyond the positives and negatives of even this verse

let your kidneys glow with hope
let your spleen become courageous
endow your children with neutronics
grow above your brain
fly the night
you are the hope of all
if you can only be true to yourself.

i know you and i love you
though you don't know me or love me
beyond the dictates of your small mind
you love me forever

ah
there is so much to say
but it is time to move on
sing another song
leave the absurd logic of circleverses

yet
i am loath
i have enjoyed it so
i have enjoyed watching you think

i do not write for me
i do not write for you
i write for a people ten thousand years from now
i write for the final child
before we evolve from this game called man

and
i write not that he may know
but that he may laugh at what we were
and chuckle at how innocent we were
and how little we pretended we knew

and
in ten thousand years
i will sit
a ghost upon the shoulder of this final child
and i will chuckle with him
for just as i am you
and you are me
he is me
and i am him
and time was all an illusion
time was just the board upon which we played

the game changes now
and it should
for why not?

we have played this game long enough
and it is time to play another
a game of golden thoughts above the mud
a game ensconced in spirit
a game which unleashes spirit
and enables us to attain the neutronic viewpoint
and achieve neutropia
and become a dream

here are my final words
are you ready?
are your ears unstopped?
your soul laid open?
your heart willing to receive the truth of me?
are you ready?
then here it is
arga barga boo

the wind

grab the wind
hold it
let it lift you like a wing
soar you to new heights

grab the wind
let it come undone in your soul

grab the wind
know the wind is in you

grab the wind
let it grab you

lift we now up
the clouds are a bath
moisture condenses the soul
playing with our eyesight at light speed

around that mountain
circle that tree
drop off that cliff
dash we down
down
to the sharp shards thousands of feet below

pull up
laugh at the spikes
that would have speared us
immobile

we cannot be immobile
for we are the wind

we are the wind

swoop through a town
around a spire
and through a belfry
over the shingles of the roofs
around the bricks of the chimneys
rattle every window and door

swoop
through each and every leaf on each and every tree
we whistle
we sing
of the wind that we are

we are the sky
and the wind is our blood
coursing over the planet entire
healing civilizations
building vast empires
going to the stars

we are the heavens
and the planets are our playground
and over the planets
like a wind
sweeps our spirit

nothing can contain us
for we are nothing
nothing but the wind

sweeping
sweeping
eternal
lifting up and putting down
there is no end to the wind

the neutronic viewpoint in circleverse

the universe is a machine.
you are a point in all directions.
the machine consists of flows,
which create forces,
which create flows,
and so on.

to handle the universe you must handle the flows.
to handle the flows you must understand
the universe flows positive and negative
and you are the neutron.

the first stage in understanding how to handle the universe
is to know
'for every action there is a reaction.'

the second stage in understanding how to handle the universe
is to know
'for something to be true, the opposite must be true.'

the third stage in understanding how to handle the universe
is to know
'do nothing until nothing is left undone.'

these are the three stages in learning how to handle the universe.
handling the universe will lead you to
the neutronic viewpoint.

how to move

i used to think i was an object
i floated through the universe
i tracked my chartless way between debris

now i know i am not an object
and i don't have trajectory
nor chart my way through trajectory

now i chart my way
not through objects as object
but
rather
i track my way as space through spaces

think
objects get in way
objects plus you or minus you
and you are swept in their path hopeless flotsam

think
you are not
therefore you are closer to space

be space
not objects
that is the secret of the universe

don't be flotsam
prone to jets and jetstreams

don't be object
be objectless
weave not as object
merely weave through space
do not magnetize yourself
merely move
by not being object

do not use time to chart your progress
rather be timeless
and chart your way unhindered

the degree to which you let go
is the degree to which you are

this is the procedure
of not being something
to be you

the more you let go
the more you go

the more you let go of having to be something
the more you can be

let the flotsam of the universe be in your path

let the universe swirl to your passing
this is the only way

think you not?
don't merely run
feel the wind
let the leaves fly
they are grateful
for your passing has given them life
they would have lain there but for your passing

so fly
let the planets orbit to your passing
don't shake them
for others must know what you know

others must not
and you must let them

else it is a lonely universe

i used to think

i was sick last year
and the year before
sick, sick, sick

but
you ask
how can someone neutronic
be sick

because he can think he is

then i realized
my universe is consecrate
it is separate
think
when i die
the universe becomes my universe
loss of flesh is loss of boundaries

so why am i sick
with boundaries

the reason is other universes
if i do nothing
if i am neutronic
then my universe is consecrate
sacred
apart
and nothing will touch

if i do something
i am open to others
realizing this
i wasn't sick

i used to think

how do you enjoy this universe
without opening
reaching
touching
and letting yourself be touched

the answer is
do right
touch right
be moral
be ethical
then your touch cannot be disputed

only good will touch he or she who is and does good

don't you remember
the universe is a machine
it is a mirror
responsive to you

the body is part of the universe
it is a mirror
do good and it will be good
feel good
and it likes it

by good
of course
i mean neutronic

good
according to man
is altruistic
bad is evil
but both are what others think

true good is neutronic
not what man thinks
not what man does
not what man is

this is a decision you must make
to achieve a consecrate universe
impervious to the touch of others

people ask you to prove it
they want to touch you
and credit good to your body
they must realize it is not your body
but you
it is nothing they can see

there is no scientific test
rather
it is in between the artifices of what man expects

how do you share?
listen
listen, listen, listen

smack, smack, smack

a child was born and spanked
why?
the doctor said to make him breath
well
maybe
maybe not

maybe he was being punished
for what?
who cares
it is the way we enter this world

there is no other

hello
smack, smack, smack

and the rest of life
smack, smack, smack

surely
there's got to be a better way

love and hold and press the chest
breath into the nostrils
set an example for life

this is the end of war
this is the end of hate
this is the end of
smack, smack, smack

such a simple thing
the act of love
holding another in pleasure
yet we withhold it
so
why?

age after age
smack, smack, smack
and we breed the rapers and malcontents
the robbers and murders
wife beaters and thugs
the ones who do wrong
and love is held silent
because inside our hearts there is only one song

smack, smack, smack

so talk to the doctors
talk to their pride
tell them to find the truth inside

talk to the fathers and the mothers as well
tell them to find a heaven not hell

and when the child misbehaves
and does the world wrong
talk to him gently and change his song

no more of the smack, smack, smack
no more of this pain we have been taught
from first breath

and when the child is grown
with children of his own
and the lessons of the past are about to be sown

no more of the
smack, smack, smack
and the future will open
and that is that

three worlds

neutropia is easy to understand
if you understand you rule
then you rule your soul

anyone can rule
if they realize that everybody rules
here is the secret on how to rule yourself

there are three worlds to be neutronicized

the body
the mind
the soul

if bodies threaten
to go positive
if they would collide
go negative

if bodies threaten to go negative
if they would separate
go positive

this first neutronization is simple
but is subject to the second neutronization

if minds threaten to go positive
if they would collide
go neutral
and let the positive be

if minds threaten to go negative
if they would separate
go neutral
and let the negative be

this is a simple matter of applying
the eleventh commandment
to its conclusion

if you don't let the positives and negatives be
you haven't applied the eleventh commandment
to its conclusion

but there is a second level
to the mind

for a mind to go positive or negative
it must first go positive or negative to itself

for a person to go positive with you
they must first go positive with themselves

for a person to go negative with you
they must first go negative with themselves

for a person to cure another
they must first cure themselves

to cure another
first cure yourself

when a person goes positive to you
go negative to yourself

when a person goes negative to you
go positive to yourself

Do the opposite and the opposite will be true

this is the truth of neutronic physics

this truth can be reached through discipline
to go further however
you need more than discipline

you need more
you need the desire
and the first level and the second level
will be subservient to the third level

when you have reached the second level
when you have reached enough people
with your anti-negative and anti-positive
then you reach everybody

when people stop going positive on you
when people stop going negative on you
then you are ready
and here is the third level

when somebody goes positive on someone else
let them

when somebody goes negative on someone else
let them

be neutronic

people wail
people moan
people fight
people cry
people band together for war
or against war
let them

apply
the eleventh commandment on this level
and let them

when the fight is over
when the damage is done
help them

don't help before
it is not your business

help after after the mistake
after the damage
for then they can learn

if you don't do this
people won't learn
and you will be the policeman
always stepping into the fight
always looking for trouble

instead
let the trouble be
and it won't come again

this is hard to apply
how do you know
when the positive or negative is agreed upon

and how do you know when it is not
life is not you must act
it is you must not act

go positive for negative
and negative for positive
to achieve neutral for positive
and neutral for negative
then you will find the third level
of the neutronic viewpoint

and all is subservient to the third level
of the neutronic viewpoint

You must strike a balance
through all your levels
if you would achieve the neutronic viewpoint

and then in the space where you be
no one will be positive
no one will be negative
for your presence is neutronic
and your presence will cure

the way will be open for others to reach
the neutronic viewpoint

the universe is a motor

whirling,
the atoms held in stasis
giving and taking charge
in a vast ebb and flow.

stepping,
up one leg and down the other
across the face of the planet
across the abyss of your dreams.

flying,
your dreams around the planet's iron core
spun to give substance
holding you to reality.

prisoner,
held in stasis
stuck in the motor
between past and future.

freedom,
is in your mind
locked in contrivances
which hold you firm.

escape,
do not run away
analyze the machine
stop letting it run you.

hope,
it is your machine
it is your contrivance
if you will just accept it.

now,
take the keys
fire up the contrivance
and remember one thing

ownership,
and you are the pirate
plundering life for its rewards
and no one to hang you

once

once i was a nazi
you were my little goat
staked out in the plains
waiting for a boat

once i smoked hasheesh
down upon my knees
the stars never looked so bright
except when i sneezed

once i held the keys
and couldn't find the lock
the door just wouldn't open
oh well

once i ruled the world
and made it my own image
but when everybody's a vampire
whose blood do you suck

once i was frightened
then i laughed
then i couldn't figure out what to do
so i did nothing

once i listened to people
the idiots became one
war was fought forever
now i am one

once there was a surge
of heavenly bliss so sweet
it wasn't mother's bosom
was it the devil's teat?

once i walked the stars
made paths where once was chaos
when i had passed on
chaos was enough

once and now forever
sung of hope in dreams
death that comes no more
nor birth

once i had a message
doesn't matter now
my fevered mind's expired
and i will follow fast

once i had an answer
now there is no other
all the questions gone
all the meditations

once i knew the truth
and the truth knew me
and the idea that i could forget
was the biggest truth of all

once i knew the lie
i pretend i have forgot
there is no pretending
not no more

poppa is a god

We are creatures bound by evolution
yet it wasn't always this way
and it doesn't have to be always this way

to a lawyer
Law is God

to a doctor
Medicine is Law

every person has this responsibility
to look
yet where does it come from

God comes from poppa
not because it is true
except to a two year old

unfortunately
many people never get over this

Many people worship poppa
all their lives

many people worship and live to be poppa
and have their time to be worshipped

I will worship and then I get to be
what I have worshipped

odd
but true and logical
after a fact

and some people outgrow poppa
lawyers outgrow poppa
doctors outgrow poppa

Scientists worship science
and spread the doctrine of technology

mathematicians worship math
and search for infinity
through the formula of math

Science means truth
and math means knowledge
yet they are viewpoints only
and not the true

So one must search without binding oneself
not by evolution,
nor by technology.

In other words
one must shed oneself of misnamed truth
and slanted doctrine

Unfortunately,
the only way to do this is to understand the doctrines
and the slanted truths
that one might progress beyond

What is beyond?
Get a lot of truths and put them together
to define the whole

define truth by gathering truths
and inspecting the whole thing

study doctrines until all align
don't stop on one
for that is to stop oneself

Do you understand?

You are not wrong for worshipping poppa.
You are not wrong for finding a slanted truth
or studying a temporary doctrine.

You must put them all together, however,
to pass beyond

I have told you enough now
the rest is up to you
Rejoice in your studies
blather your doctrine
trade with others
but put it all together

the truth waits
The neutronic truth

what is your worth?

what are you worth?
what do you cost?
what is the value of you?

it's easy to figure out if you do it right
but the answer may not be what you like

all you have to do is ask yourself
these three questions

do you waste?
do you maintain?
do you make?

do you waste your time and opportunity
do you waste your friends
do you squander the good will
that is aimed towards you

do you work
but let others do the work for you
do you play and hog the ball

do you have to be the center of attention
instead of enjoying all those around you

do you waste
are you a waste

Or...
do you maintain
helping the status quo
helping things remain as they are

do you maintain peace no matter the cost
do you sacrifice your worth that everybody gets along

do you work at being responsible
reasonable
diligent and always kind

Fool
you are a victim of life

Or...
do you make
do you make friends
or enemies if you wish?

do you make fun no matter the cost?
do you make work
and then clean up your mess?

do you make stuff
and jobs
and value for all?

are you the one that people look to
when they need somebody to look to?

are you willing to hurt as well as help?
are you able to balance the good and the bad?
are you able to be by yourself?

able to take the insults
the jibes
the ill will of those
who envy you your freedom

And it is freedom

freedom of mind
the ability to see choices
and then actually make them

the freedom of direction
ultimately
the freedom to make directions for all

what you are is you

not bound by waste
not trapped by the need to maintain
but knowing life changes
and that it changes only as you change

you are a maker

money is god

Mankind is a suit
but who is wearing it?

Who is in charge of taking it to the cleaners?

I know,
sounds silly,
but listen…

workers are the shoes on which this society walks

politicians are the hat and ring and necklace

And that bauble over there,
that is the artist

that set of brass knuckles is the military

every piece of mankind can be described in this way
so comes the question
who's in charge?

everybody is in charge of their lives
somewhat
but who is in charge of the whole?

not the politicians
they are the mouthpieces for a society gone bad

not the military
for they are a solution when the mouthpieces fail

not the religious leaders
for they may show the way but it is only
who they show the way to that matters

who is in charge?
well,
my friend
I hate to say it
but the wallet is in charge

the society got badly skewed
and screwed
many years ago

money got put in charge
people make decisions not on what is best
but what makes them money
people make decisions based on their wallet

this is not the way it is supposed to be

this is people reacting to what they have
instead of making plans for what they want life to be

the bankers are interesting sharks

money is their god
and they squeeze the wallet
merely to perpetuate money

money
a symbol for energy
a way to store up one day's work
so as to use it on another day

how is that god?

yet,
the bankers believe it so
and they encourage all to believe it
and fill their coffers

They are high priests
and money is their god

how do you stop worshipping money
it is easy
simply stop

do not buy before you have the money
plan your life so you have the money
live life and not money
stop being a slave

when you buy,
don't buy until you have twice the price in your wallet

never empty your wallet

to tell the bill collector that you have no money
when it is stuffed
is not a sin

yes
pay all your debts
but only to ten per cent more
not to ten per cent
per cent
per cent
forever
and ever
until you have repaid the loan
twenty times
and are dead

pay only to ten per cent then cut it off
listen to the buzzards scream
as they try to savage you to dead meat

the uproar will die and life will go on
and don't go into debt again

instead
don't buy until you have twice the money in your wallet

avoid moneylenders like the plague
for they are a plague

they are skewed
and believe that money is god

the only way to handle them
the right way to handle them
is to avoid borrowing money
and shun the moneylenders
in business and in life
and in government

let the scavengers root amongst ashes
it is all they deserve for skewing mankind

those who attack

There are those who say that you can't
These are the ones who haven't

Man doesn't know why he is
he justifies himself by creating structures to contain himself

These structures are traps
but a man can be untrapped
he doesn't need to justify his existence

man can just be

There are people without imagination
they are frightened by those with imagination
it shakes the structure that supports their reason for being

To live is to create
to create structures is good
to be trapped by what you have created is bad

Better to be
to live to create
and if those who are trapped attack
let them
they are justifying their own trap

and the ones who listen
who grab the structure and shake
who ask why it is
they are the ones who will escape the trap

they are the ones who deserve you
forget the others
their time is not yet
and someone else must free them

now is your time

the moon from the mountain

The moon from the mountain wreathed in clouds,
flickering over the eyes illuminates the soul.
It is no different than the moon as viewed from the prison cell.
Trap the body and free the soul.

For when the body is laid down
the eyes are closed and the spirit dreams forth
sees reality for what it is
travels through the thickest substance
as if it were nothing.

When the body is held motionless
that which is motionless shall go forth
the spirit shall soar and travel
through the changing realms of the universe
without cease nor trouble.

Your only enemy is the man who says no
The negative ones shall not go free
and do not want you to
for it shows the lie that they are
Misery loves company

Even the lowest criminal is free
if he does one thing
forgive
forgive self
forgive others
forgive
when all is forgiven
no binds hold
and the spirit shall soar

During your time on earth
build your body strong
make your mind sharp
and when the time comes to not be on earth
the robust discipline and the sharp intellect will understand
and be free

dreams are the source of hell

Dreams are the source of hell
or so the corruptionists would have you believe

Have no dreams
and you will never leave slavery

Have dreams
and the corruptionist will seek you out
and spite you until death

They are so jealous

Their dreams are built of bricks
and the bricks are made of money
so they toss themselves into the deepest ocean
and never sees the light of themselves

A man who knows
that money is a measurement of energy understands
and cannot be trapped
cannot be killed
cannot be enslaved.

The man who knows this truth
merely makes more money

The man who knows this truth will never be empty
the corruptionist will never be full
the prisoner will never dream
the dreamer will never be in prison

to wake

To wake
it is to wake
it is why we went to sleep
to wake

thus
walking through this world unawake
we search for why we should be awake
what is the purpose of life?
why am I here?
are these not the questions of the amnesiac?

Are these not the questions of the sleeper
attempting to undream himself?
to shed the flesh?
to rend the trappings?
to let loose the spirit?
to let loose that which can't be seen?

I cannot be seen nor heard nor felt by any sense.
I am invisible
a ghost hidden in flesh
a spirit bound
something that is not thing

I am not thing
I am not of this universe
I am not

I am not substance nor material
but only the illusion of such

I am not an animal nor a man
nor even some evolved species

I am not
and before I wasn't
I was an I am

Now
I am again
I am an I am all over again
Reborn
having sunk so low
that I finally may climb
to the truth of myself
I am

Yet there are those still asleep
still hold to the substance of the universe
as if it was them
and they expect me to believe the same
as if an object
could control a thought

the only thought
one can control
is the I am
and
after that
one may control the universe
but not before having that thought

Yea
though I walk through the valley of sleep
I shall fear not the sleepers
for they shall awake
and they shall be as I am

I Am...forever (part one)

This universe dies every day
every part
forever
but i do not

i am forever
i am the spark in the night
the immortal vision
the spirit
the soul
the I am
the awareness that never dies

i change bodies like suits of clothes
trading lives
one life a clown
another a hero
still another...a murderer

i change and the universe changes
it is my blackboard
my playpen
my existence

Stop the universe
and i have no place to be

so the universe continues
it turns
it dazzles for me
and I forget I made it
so as to immerse myself
in my existence
purely

stop me...
but you can't
you can stop my body
but the I am that i am will always be

a new body
a new play
a new revenge
a new day

i continue making the universe
turning the days
immortal i am
immortal
and the universe dies for me

I Am...forever (part two)

I am unhinged in time
most men aren't
but i am

i can not forget that i am immortal
that i am mortal in body only
i can not forget that the universe is not me
i can not forget to be aware

i can not forget to remember the future

i can forget the past
until the past no longer holds me

i can forget the universe
and so am able to see it beyond
what it is

would you like to remember that which comes?
would you like to remember that which you created
and then forgot you created?

the turns of life about to be revolved?
the blue of skies yet to come?

it is easy
just look at now and forget
forget the universe for it isn't real
it is just a figment of your fevered imagination

forget who everybody thinks you are
forget who you are called
forget all those temporary things
forget until you forget yourself
and all the things you think are you

for they didn't make you
you made them
and they are temporary
mere whimseys of your imagination

you are beyond
all that you think you are
you are beyond
and your true ability is...
imagination

my real flesh

the most terrible thing in the universe
is a man who doesn't know himself

doesn't know where he comes from,
doesn't know why he is
doesn't know what he is
doesn't know who he is
and has no reason for existence

he has no purpose
he works at low jobs
stifling his high dreams
that is terrible

man bangs around
going from trouble to tragedy
having an occasional good moment
wondering at the accident of his birth

then he finds a discipline
maybe yoga or religion
maybe my preference
martial arts

he works,
disciplines himself
and learns about himself
he learns about his body
and what it can do
he learns about his mind
about his emotions
and he starts to take control
one day
his training at a peak
he might be standing on a mountain
or in a desert
or on a boat in the ocean
but he's looking around
and suddenly he sees himself

oh!
he looks at the moon
or a mountain
or a cloud in the sky
and he thinks:
'oh
there I am'
idle thoughts drop to the side
and he sees the sunset
and the sunrise
and he knows:
i am not flesh
nor emotion
i am everything i perceive
that is the true me
that is who i am
that is my real flesh

to run in the great race
to build monuments to self
to endeavor to persevere...
that is the illusion of life
but this life
this universe
this is our true flesh
the constituency of our thoughts

we hem ourselves in
trap ourselves
and think the flesh is true
it is not

flesh is the motor scooter of our short lives
the universe is our home
and we move it with our thoughts
that is our long life
our forever life

neutronically speaking

there is
in this universe
only motion
the results of this motion are only
force or flow

all forces and flows must emanate from you

or other i ams

The structure of the universe is a motor

there are two poles
between which are forces and flows

from atoms to galaxies
this is true

even when there are more than two
you can break it down to two

indeed
when there is chaos and confusion
simply
find one other i am
and deal with that other i am
and watch chaos and confusion disappear

All the problems of life can be resolved
and dissolved
when you find one other i am

The question then becomes
how?

You know who
so how?

to solve is simple
neutronically speaking.

simply understand:
there are three possible motions

to go towards is protonic
to go away is electronic
to maintain distance is neutronic

find another i am

are they coming towards you?
are they protonic?

are they going away from you?
are they electronic?

are they holding distance in stasis?
are they neutronic?

holding distance is stable
holding distance creates stability.
holding distance creates neutronicity.

to go away is okay
unless you want to go towards

and the opposite is also true

to go towards is okay
unless you want to go away

to move in a direction
you must align desire with motion

do not go away
when you want to go towards
do not go towards
when you want to go away

if you want to go towards
go towards
And
if you want to go away
go away

being aligned in this fashion will create your neutronicity.

to create motion without being aligned
causes misalignment in the motor of the universe
and you can't move the universe unless you are aligned
so it is best to be neutronic

to understand this concept
you must understand that emotion is motion inside the head.

to be neutronic you must not have motion inside the head.
motion inside the head misaligns you

we are not talking about motion like happiness or joy
for those are satisfactions of the soul

we are talking about anger and fear
and so on
motion inside the head that makes you unhappy
is what we are talking about.

you can always find a motion
that will resolve the motion inside your head

fear?
the desire to go away?
go away and it never resolves.
go towards and it will resolve

anger?
the desire to go towards?
go towards and it never resolves
go away and it never resolves

remain in stasis
holding your position
maintaining your distance
all will resolve

there are always three choices
to go towards
to go away
to maintain distance

and these three choices must be aligned
even inside your head

that being said
let us take a case

bob has motion inside his head.
he would go towards tom and kill him

but he doesn't want to get dirty
and besides
tom is bigger than him

but bob gives in to the motion inside his head.
he pulls a gun and pulls a trigger

tom
dull fellow
didn't see the motion inside bob's head.
now
seeing the motion of the gun
he becomes undull
and he must make a choice

if he runs towards he becomes a bigger target
If he runs away he becomes a smaller target
but
in an oddity of neutronicity
becoming smaller
he is becomes stable in the sights of bob

third choice
move sideways and the bullet misses
move sideways again
misses

but there is a problem
tom knows that eventually
bob will not miss
moving sideways only
does not make for eternal missings

so tom moves sideways and away
eventually the distance is so great
bob will always miss
and tom can get his own gun
hopefully a longer gun

in this case tom solved by going away,
but eventually he will have to go towards
and stop the motion inside bob's head
an ounce of lead stops motion admirably

and when one terminal is not moving
there is not the stasis
necessary to continue living

you may not like this example
but I say this:
you can continue being a liberal if your heart doesn't bleed

let's take another example

aunt Daisy says
'mow the lawn for a dollar'

you have motion inside your head
greed for the dollar
but you don't want to mow the lawn

problem
to go towards the dollar

means going towards the lawn
unless you lie
you could create motion inside your head by lying

tell aunt daisy you mowed the lawn
take the dollar and go away
she's half blind
can't remember what's in her purse
heck
you could tell her she needs her lawn mowed tomorrow
and do it all again

isn't that nicer than shooting people?
aren't you glad i came up with this example?

lucky you.

but I forgot to tell you
aunt daisy is married to uncle bob
uh oh
uncle bob has motion inside his head
and he's got extra motion inside his head
because he missed tom

maybe you should go towards the lawn after all.
or
the heck with it
go away from lawn and dollar both

okay
problems
problems
problems
want to know how to have no problems?

easy
pay attention now
and I will tell you how to live a life with no problems
get ready
here it is…
virtue armors the soul

do good
direct the motion inside your head
make it stop
you become impervious
even to uncle bob

there are dozens of virtues
and each one protects your ability to motion
and eases the motion inside your head

patience
don't go towards or away
even inside your head
those you help will become competent

tolerance when others scream hate
inject a correcting motion into the hate
it will stop going towards ignorance and destruction

kindness
a random act a day
keeps uncle bob away
and so on

make a list of virtues
write examples of how to break and how to make
this will inject virtue into the motor of the universe
and make your passage possible
and even profitable

for people unlike uncle bob will come to you
and give to you what you need

remember...
virtue armors the soul

as is my wont

Someday I'll lay there
tired of the jello and the bedpans
tired of the visitors who smile
and don't know what to say

I'll look back at my life
wish I could tell them
what fun it was
to laugh every day

I'll stare at the ceiling
and let the nurses pass by
ignoring me as is their wont
as I lay and wait to die

There is no pain
I don't mind the drugs
I don't mind the senses dulled
I don't mind

I lose my mind
the memories lose me
I watch as the ceiling comes closer
my body stretching out

unable to contain me
unable to hold the spirit of the days
unable to restrain the wild spirit
that is I

The texture of the ceiling is paint
white
I can't figure out how
to turn and look downwards

The long beep turns me
and a nurse turns it off
I am looking down now
and seeing the peace of me

They will come now
and take my body away
leaving me stuck to this ceiling
until I remember

how do you move without a body
how do you talk without a voice
how do you express your zest
how do you make a choice

I watch myself
I study my face
I think of how I am not now
but will always be

people come
last rites
crying
but why

I am not longer infirm
trapped held
prisoner
of my own will

I am free
as soon as i remember
to think backwards
is to move what I am now

a point in all directions
the back of my head
no longer stops me
from seeing in all directions

now I must be the moon
I must visit space
and be the stars
and someday

someday
I will be human again
I will be born a baby
and conveniently forget

who I am
what I am
a point in all directions
forever

creating the universe
as is my wont
trapping myself for fun
and calling it a body

someday
I will come again
I will live
and see you again

until that day
look to the stars
watch me wheel the heavens
watch me

for somewhere
somehow
always
I will be watching you

conclusion

Goodbye

The author created a science called Neutronics.
If you have the stomach for world changing philosophy,
look for…

A soul changing look at what the universe is,
what life is,
what you are.

Al Case

not your corporate writer...
but a REAL storyteller,
a rogue writer!

Find him now at...

AlCaseBooks.com